ISBN-13: 9798366648998

Cover design by: Rachel Langston, KC Misulis, Sophiko Lagvilava

TABLE OF CONTENTS

HOW TO USE THIS BOOK

This book is a collection of ideas from the brains at Misulis Group. MG is oriented on helping people find a job that leaves them fulfilled and fits in with their lifestyle. We are employee-focused and aim to provide the tools you need to get the career of your dreams. From information and advice on navigating the corporate environment, to one on one career advising and coaching, we have the tools to get you started down the path to your future success. This book acts as a guide in three parts.

- Section 1: Investing In Yourself
- Section 2: How To Get Started
- Section 3: Once You Get There, How To Be Happy
- About The Authors

The first section is dedicated to investing in yourself and helping you find motivation to jump into today's job market. Learn how to find a career you like and set the goals to get there. Use this book to develop a personal pitch that will get you in the door.

The second section is getting started. Go through a guide for your personal documents, with tips and tricks from industry professionals. Get advice from CEO KC Misulis on how to break into a new industry and learn the psychology behind making better decisions.

The third section is dedicated to keeping you happy at the job you find. This section is full of advice for dealing with difficult situations, unreasonable people, and crabby workplace grumps. Don't let that bully boss or crazy work expectations take you down! We here at MG know that you have the ability to do great work, and we want to help you get there. We hope you enjoy the collection of essays and feel free to reach out if you like our ideas and want to interact more.

SECTION 1: INVESTING IN YOURSELF

The Power Of Goal Setting - Christie Hawking

Why Strategic Planning Is Vital To Achieving Your Goals And Why Consulting An Expert Can Help.

Have you ever said to yourself or someone else that you will achieve something, but seemingly, it hasn't quite happened yet? Maybe that something is still an actual goal of yours, but you are stuck with what you can do to achieve it. Don't worry. We have all been there, and most of us still have a bunch of things we want to achieve but are either too distracted, not motivated enough, or just not sure how to go about it. Whatever the barrier, sometimes a little help is required to get you back on track or even help you create the path you need from the get-go.

What Is Goal Setting?

A goal is a future-oriented objective that is sought to be achieved. Goal setting is the strategic, deliberate plan on how you get there. It involves a sequence of reasonable smaller goals or steps that guide a person towards their desired outcome. Funnily enough, the act of goal setting is the first stage to achieving any goal one might want to achieve.

What Types Of Goals Require Goal Setting?

"Anything in life worth having doesn't come easy" is a common phrase that can usually be associated with the type of goals we are discussing here. However, no matter the "thing," the critical difference between a goal and a momentary intention is that a goal will not come naturally and requires you to put in some effort. And guess what, that "effort" is in the form of directed smaller goals written out as time-sensitive milestones or deadlines.

Why Consulting A Strategic Planning Expert Can Help You Achieve Your Goals – Career Or Otherwise?

Knowing how to set goals and create a strategic plan is a skill. Most of the time, we use this skill naturally in everyday life when planning basic things, like cooking, scheduling a day, or general day-to-day tasks. But we sometimes get a bit lost regarding more ambitious goals, short or long-term careers, or lifestyles. This is because a lot of the time, goals of this nature that do exist outside of our immediate reality, are subject to our imagination. The great thing about goals like this is that there are infinite ways to achieve them – the not-so-great thing is that it requires us to differentiate between reasonable and unreasonable.

That's why consulting an expert can help – even the most reasonable person can sometimes make unreasonable goals.

An expert in strategic planning can teach you how to evaluate your goals, big and small. They will help you redefine what is possible to achieve and what you want, and provide an objective perspective so a reasonable, time-appropriate strategy can be created.

Why You Can't Find A Career You Like And What To Do About It – Eliana Silbermann

Growing up, you were asked the same rotten, unhelpful, no-good question at least 100,002 times a year. "What do you want to be when you grow up?" If you were like most kids, you always had an answer prepared—ideally, a career in mind with high status or heroic and very important. But now you're an adult. And you're struggling to decide on a career. Why?

You can't find a career you like because your childhood dream is not your dream job. Like all humans, you have competing needs and desires, and having a so-called "boring" job is seen as slacking off or lacking ambition. Most childhood career dreams are built on shaky ground. Even if your mum or dad had the job you thought you'd love, how much detail did they give you? Maybe the highlights or a general overview. And if no one close to you had that job, you'll know even less.

No one tells a young aspiring veterinarian they'll need to be emotionally strong enough to accept not saving every animal. Or that they'll need to put down some of their adorable fluffy patients.

If you say you want to be a vet because you love animals, you rarely get a long list of possible careers—except maybe zookeeper and dog trainer —which you may or may not like more. Maybe you'd enjoy being a cat behaviourist or having a job taking care of lab mice.

You grow up to find you don't want the career you thought you wanted. Now you don't know what career you want.

It's even worse if you worked for your entire childhood, adolescence, and maybe even early adulthood towards this career path because you suffer from what psychologists call **Identity Foreclosure**. This means you are committed to an identity without exploring options. You never experimented with your identity before establishing one based on the choices or values of other people.

For example, when adults expect an answer to that rotten, unhelpful, no-good question, "What do you want to be when you grow up?" (It's not really their fault. They didn't know any better and were trying their best.) But that's not the only reason. You have competing needs and desires

Like every human being on Earth (and the people spread across the galaxy if our descendants ever get there), you're complicated. You want and need things, many of which clash with each other.

Suppose an amazing new nonprofit organization offered you a job, but they can't pay you enough to cover your rent. And children are expensive. (Seriously, kids seem to grow out of their new shoes within two days. You fed them three whole times today, but you need to feed them again tomorrow. And the next day. For 18 years.) Popular blogger Tim Urban describes the situation like this:

> *"Some motivations have conflicting interests with others, you cannot, by definition, have everything you want. Going for one thing you want means, by definition, not going for others, and sometimes, it'll specifically mean going directly against others."*

Your Dream Job Might Be A "Boring" Job

The checklist of what makes the perfect career is different for everyone. Some people want a career based on their passions. For them, "find something you love, and you'll never work a day in your life" is absolutely 100% true. It's not true for everyone. It might not be true for you. We're taught that having a job which society considers boring or in an industry that society considers boring is settling. That it's almost a failure.

Not trying to climb the career ladder to the top means you're considered a slacker or unambitious. These are supposed to be bad things.

Even if we'd be miserable as managers or simply not suited to the responsibilities, we're expected to aim for a promotion. We're told we should be going for the next shiny, higher-status, higher-power title. And we're told everyone dreams of having more status and more power. *You might like a career that simply pays you enough for your lifestyle, gives you enough work-life balance to pursue your hobbies, and isn't too stressful.*

That's okay. Not every passion needs to be monetized. You can create rock music without trying to become a star.

We're Trained To Focus On The Most Exciting Career Roles And The Most Exciting Companies.

Meanwhile, you might be happier working as a salesperson at Dunder Mifflin than an engineer at SpaceX. You just haven't considered it. So, what should you do? Ask yourself if you're willing to pay the price, not just the financial cost. Are you willing to dedicate a decade of your life, gallons of skull sweat to study your textbooks, and long tiring nights to become a surgeon? Or whatever the equivalent is for the profession you're interested in. Be honest with yourself. Are you willing to take on the downsides, sacrifices, and pain associated with that career choice? Not just willing, but almost enjoying the price?

Don't forget opportunity costs. You can't spend the time, money, and effort you put towards becoming a surgeon on becoming an accountant, just like if you go out to a diner for dinner, you can't spend the same money and time ordering a pizza and eating it at home.

Start with what you don't want. Humans have a strange quirk. Often, we know much more about what we don't want. We can spend days making lists of it. I'm sure there are careers you know immediately you won't like. So, start here. Think about why you lack interest in those careers. Go beyond the surface. Do they require you to make split-second decisions, but do you prefer thoroughly evaluating the situation before responding? Do you prefer getting a result that's either correct or incorrect, with zero ambiguity? Write it down. Use it to evaluate your career options.

Your Pitch - Sophiko Lagvilava

Are you a job hunter? Do you want to change the industry? In this case, you need your personal pitch to shine in the interview and get the life you deserve.

What Is A Personal Pitch?

Your pitch, also known as an **elevator pitch**, gives a concise overview of our experience and skills as a candidate. You should aim for it to be about a minute in length and focus on the 3-5 key messages you'd want someone to remember. We use personal pitch when speaking about our career or aspirations, which effectively demonstrates our professional aptitude, strengths, and skills.

What Is An 'Elevator Pitch'?

We use 'Elevator Pitch' in the same way. Imagine that we are in an elevator with a hiring manager of a company we would love to work for, and we have the length of the elevator ride to convince them to give us an interview.

So, we have 30-60 seconds, roughly 75 words, to provide a clear, concise, and impactful overview of ourselves.

Why Do We Need A Personal Pitch?

Every job hunter should have a tremendous personal pitch that can catch someone's attention and stand out from the crowd of potential candidates. You must reassure them that you have the skills they need. Help them understand your motivations for change. Show your commitment to your new industry. Everything we do has to be better than a candidate with industry experience.

Where Do We Use Personal Pitches?

There are many uses for personal pitches, including in a cover letter. Use your elevator pitch to either help you brainstorm the main points you want to touch upon in your letter or use it within the actual text of your statement to start off strong. During an interview hiring managers will ask you to tell them about yourself. Having an honest, memorable, and well-thought-out answer can capture their attention and show that you know the value you can offer their organization.

At networking events you're likely to meet dozens, if not hundreds, of people. Having an authentic statement about yourself at the ready can help break the ice when starting a conversation. On Social Media use your Pitch to help build your personal brand on LinkedIn and other professional networks.

How Do We Write An Excellent Personal Pitch?

Your pitch should be finished in 30-60 seconds and contain 3 to 5 key messages - 75% from previous experience and career history, and 25% population for the future. What to say in your pitch? Your elevator speech should be brief and persuasive. You are sharing your skills. Don’t forget to be positive and mention your goals. Research your audience, and speak to them. Look at their eyes, not in a weird way. Friendly and happy but not forced. What should you not say? Don't speak too fast and avoid rambling. Don't frown or speak in a monotone way or restrict yourself to a single elevator pitch.

Key Takeaways

Keep it short and sweet. Your Pitch is a sales pitch. Be sure you can deliver your message in 60 seconds or less. Focus on the essentials. Say who you are, what you do, and what you want to achieve. Be positive and persuasive. Your time is limited. Focus on what you want to do, not what you don't want to do. Be upbeat and flexible. Practice is important. Deliver your speech to a friend or record it so that you can be sure that your message is clear. It seems strange and awkward, but practicing out loud works. The more often we practice our Personal Pitch, the more natural it will sound and the more confident we will present it.

Elevator Pitch Examples:

Context: Seeking a job opportunity Job Title: Communications "Hi, I'm Kate. I've spent the last eight years learning and growing in my role as a Communication Specialist at a nonprofit organization, where I've developed and optimized strategic communication and media plans for our organization and managed activities for various projects as a Team Leader. One of my proudest achievements is an 'Information Media Tour' in five major cities in the country and a 'Job Fair.' I've been interested in moving to an international organization for a while, and I really like your company in the education field. I could do a lot for you. Could you please tell me about any communication and social media planning needs you may have in your team?"

SECTION 2: HOW TO GET STARTED

Personal Profile Documents - Christie Hawking

In today's job market, the Personal Profile Document has become the number one requirement that potential employers request. Before an employer takes valuable time to interview you, they want to meet you – on paper or in digital space. How you impress that employer with your resume can, and will, make all the difference. Without Profile Documents, you can't even begin to compete, and an inferior resume will quickly eliminate you before you even have a fighting chance. That is why it is imperative to have a superior resume that effectively lets employers know what you can do for them.

In the land of job opportunities, having a top-notch, eye-catching resume with perfect formatting, job-specific buzzwords, and a draw-the-reader-instantly personal pitch is the difference between an open and closed door. Let's not forget about the cover letter, which requires even more customization when applying for jobs. On top of this, you must figure out how to get past the ever-evolving advancements in Applicant Tracking Software (ATS) that can either filter you in or out in a second.

All this ultimately means is that the days of HR personnel or recruiters spending hours reviewing and analyzing first-stage applications are no more. The actual contents of your resume, cover letter, or any other personal document mean more now than they ever did in the past. Of course, you can get around this by knowing someone on the inside or only applying for jobs at smaller companies, but why limit yourself to that when you can use our expertise to help future-proof your personal documents so they can be used anywhere and pass the computerized eyes of ATS systems. Let's look at these elements a bit closer.

What are some types of personal profile documents? These days, personal promotion is everything, and this is why you commonly find that companies are asking for more in terms of personal profile documents to gauge a candidate personally and professionally.

Some of these documents include:

- Resume (CV)
- Cover letter or motivation letter
- Personal Pitch
- Personal website
- LinkedIn Profile
- Professional portfolio (especially for creative roles)

Sometimes companies are even removing the need for these documents and instead asking you to manually fill in online applications with all corresponding personal information. This makes it even more imperative that the contents of your actual personal profile documents be transferable in these circumstances. Not only will this save you a lot of time, but you can feel confident in the content you provide.

What Is ATS, And What Does It Look For?

Applicant tracking software (ATS) essentially organizes, filters, ranks, and collects information on prospective job applicants, mostly from their resumes but in some instances in other documents. Depending on the ATS deployed, it will generally be analyzing and looking for job-specific keywords, synonyms of skills, font type, abbreviations, and even overall formatting of your documents.

Why Is Having A Solid LinkedIn Important?

If you don't have a LinkedIn account, you're most likely missing out on countless opportunities you didn't even know were possible. If you do have a LinkedIn profile but aren't seeming to get any traction when you apply for jobs, then it's clear your profile needs a revamp ASAP. LinkedIn uses ATS software to recommend high-quality candidates to recruiters and employers, even if you haven't applied for a role specifically. This means that opportunities can come to you any time of day.

Why Is Linkedin Essential In Today's World?

LinkedIn is the largest professional networking website. It helps you to create and manage your online professional brand, which means nearly an unlimited supply of network connections and job opportunities. As a candidate, you can use LinkedIn to research companies. At the same time, you will also appear in the search done by different recruiters. Here your presence on LinkedIn plays a significant role. If you are a job seeker, you can let recruiters and your network on LinkedIn know you are open to new job opportunities. LinkedIn will help your profile appear in search results when recruiters look for suitable job candidates.

Four Reasons Why LinkedIn Is Important For Getting A Job - Sophiko Lagvilava

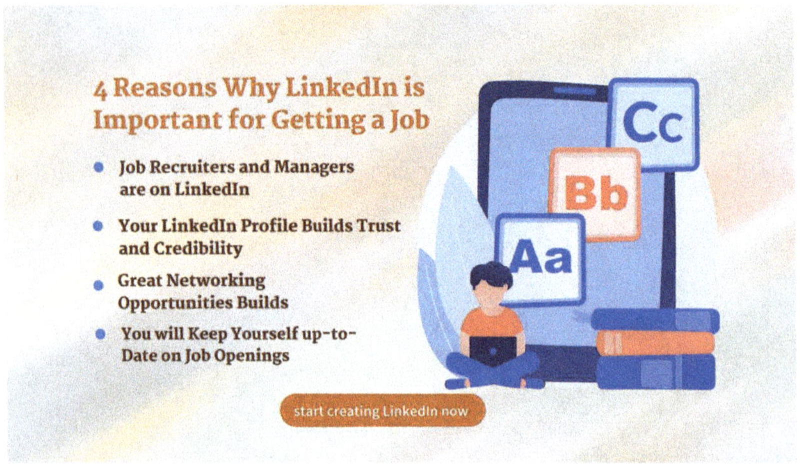

LinkedIn provides valuable information about companies, interview tips, and professional networking opportunities to benefit current employees looking for that next big move and those fresh on the job market. The primary benefit of LinkedIn is the ability to create a professional profile that you can then make visible to recruiters, HR professionals, and other people in your industry.

LinkedIn offers plenty of opportunities for those on the job market, helping them form connections, keep track of businesses and events, and even get job-seeking done. There are four main reasons why every job seeker should be on LinkedIn.

Job Recruiters and Managers are on LinkedIn.

The website can help you find a job faster because most hiring managers and recruiters already use it. Having an active and well-put-together LinkedIn profile will significantly increase the chances of your discovery by companies looking to hire people based on your skills and experience. In other words, potential employers will contact you if they think you will be a good fit for their organization, instead of you having to look at and contact each company actively.

Your LinkedIn Profile Builds Trust and Credibility.

A well-written profile will give you credibility and establish you as a trustworthy potential employee. Every time a recruiter contacts you, you can be sure that they've looked at your profile. Your LinkedIn profile will act as a validator because you are a real person, not someone whose CV or resume is too good to be true.

LinkedIn offers you an excellent opportunity to network with other professionals in your field.

And the faster you start this networking, the better it will be down the line. Regardless of whether you are currently working, you can make use of your network of connections if you are looking for other employment.

You will keep yourself up-to-date on job openings.

With a LinkedIn account, you will be able to continually keep an eye out for various job opportunities that will interest you. The overwhelming majority of companies will post any job openings that they may have, and you can keep track of these in real time.

A LinkedIn profile will greatly help you land your dream job. And the sooner you have it, the better it will be for your career.

Advice From H. R. – Rachel Langston

Finding a job can be challenging. Finding a job with good pay, competitive benefits, and a comfortable work-life balance can feel impossible. If filling out application after application and never getting a call back is an all too common struggle for you, listen up! At Misulis Group, we are always looking for ways to stay on the cutting edge of corporate culture and provide the most up-to-date advice to our clients. We met with HR extraordinaire Ella from The Public Good Projects to talk about the hiring process from the other side of the desk. Ella got down and detailed with job seeking in the current market, the hiring process through the eyes of HR, and simple tips to bump you up – or down – on the list of potential new hires.

The Public Good Projects, or PGP, is a public health non-profit that serves local communities through projects and initiatives. Ella is their Senior Manager of People Experiences, meaning she handles all HR and the initial stages of the hiring process. As a stay-at-home mom working remotely while taking care of my kiddo, the first thing I had to ask Ella about was remote work. Remote or work-from-home jobs are a hot commodity. Since the pandemic, it seems like everyone is looking for ways to continue working from home as more and more companies are pushing workers back to the office.

How Is Hiring For A Fully Remote Organization Different From A More Traditional Work Environment?

"I don't have any problem connecting with people through the screen, but that's not the case for everyone. It can be challenging if someone is naturally introverted or more reserved."

The Public Good Projects is a 100% remote working environment, so Ella has some valuable insight into the hiring processes for remote positions. According to her, a unique challenge faced in the remote working environment is how difficult it can be to connect over a computer. Most people know a connection is necessary for an interview to go well, but that's a little more difficult through a Zoom, Teams, or phone call. We tend to be more withdrawn over a video call than in person, so don't let the screen hold you back. If connecting with people is not your forte, try to loosen up and be more open in the virtual meeting space. Work to be more relaxed and dynamic when speaking, use inviting body language, and don't be afraid to laugh a little. Serious and professional are not synonyms. This awkwardness can be two-sided, so remember that your interviewer could also struggle with this. Having more experience with the interview process doesn't mean they can't feel uncomfortable over the phone or through the screen.

PGP is a smaller organization and does not employ AI resume scanning software. Ella reviews each resume herself and decides who gets to be in the *maybe* pile and who doesn't make the cut. She shared her thought process while sorting and some tips to ensure your resume doesn't get immediately thrown in the trash. Her advice to get noticed was surprisingly simple. What are the most common mistakes candidates make while applying for a job? "The most common thing I see is resumes and cover letters with spelling and grammar mistakes." Make sure that your resume is written correctly and proofread it. Lazy editing, poor spelling, and simple grammar mistakes indicate to the hiring manager that an applicant doesn't care. A lazy resume is also an indication of your future work. No company wants to hire someone too lazy to double-check their work. So, if you don't want an immediate rejection, run it through spellcheck.

Another common flaw that Ella sees is incomplete or incorrect applications. If the cover letter is missing or addressed to the wrong company, it's a clear sign that you don't care. Make sure you personalize your cover letter to the job and that all the details are correct. When you write a cover letter, be specific. Reference work experience on your resume and connect it to the current role. Note the reasons for any gaps in your resume so they don't have to hunt for answers. Talk about what you know about the company and why you want to work there.

PGP is a health communications organization, so Ella often looks for some explanation or connection to the organization's mission. If you don't care about public health, you probably are not a good fit. It doesn't mean you are automatically out if you don't have the exact qualifications they want. Include detail on why you feel like you would be a good fit for the company and what strengths you can bring to the table. If you lack the experience, address that in your cover letter and tell them how your limited experience shouldn't disqualify you because you have transferrable skills. Your application is their first introduction to you as a potential employee, so make your first impression good. Take the time to reread your application before you hit submit. Make sure you have everything they asked for, answer all the questions, and work to show them why you are interested.

What Advice Do You Have For People Searching For A Job In Our Current Job Market?

"It's an employees market right now, don't give up."

What if you followed all her tips and still didn't get the job? The best thing to do is keep looking. There are lots of openings now, and companies need good help. Take the time to personalize each resume and cover letter for the position, double-check everything, then let your experience speak for itself. Don't get demotivated because you aren't the right fit for a few companies.

Breaking Into A New Industry – K. C. Misulis

"You need 3-5 years of experience for an entry-level job". This is a common joke in 2022, and I am sad to say that this is true. Hirers know they have the advantage over job seekers, so they hire overqualified people and don't have to train them. But if you are coming out of college, that really sucks because there seems to be no way to break that barrier. So how do we break that 3-5 years of experience gap? Assuming nepotism isn't an option, giving yourself that job is best.

It sounds weird, but the fact of the matter is that if you want to experience doing a job that you're not qualified for, it's better for you to have your own small unincorporated business than to spend hours and hours at the job application slot machine. So let's say Luna wants to become a plumber. She could try to apply to a bunch of jobs, but all her resume is going to say is that she's been reading tarot cards, casting spells, and making animated explainer videos. It's very unlikely that this is going to work. Or, she can declare that she has founded the "Cat and Moon Plumbing Company," make herself a logo in Canva, make sure she has the tools she needs, then look around at family and friends who have plumbing issues.

Now, because Luna is new, and we don't quite trust her yet, she'll probably have to do *some* work for free or at a discount. But over time, she can start asking for money to get paid for this. Not only that, once she's done this for a while, her resume now says that she's been working at Cat and Moon

Plumbing Company for this time! Do you see how that works? If she wanted to be a corporate executive, it's the same concept. She reframes it as now she's the CEO of Cat and Moon Plumbing Company. Or project management if she took on a big plumbing project.

Now I hear your question: Is this legitimate? Isn't Luna just making this all up and is now going to jail because she lied on her resume? The answer is that this is totally okay! Because this is actually how small business works! If Luna was so successful in her one-cat plumbing business that she hired other plumbers to take on other jobs, she now has created jobs and has a solid small business. Even if she didn't create a great business and took on jobs for friends and family for basically nothing, that's okay too. Because it's still real-world experience, and she tried to build a start-up from scratch. Either way, her resume is much better, and she's much more likely to get those jobs in the future.

So if you want to break that barrier and aren't quite sure how just give yourself that job, it's not a magic solution, and you're going to have to learn a lot about running a small organization, but the fact of the matter is that you don't need *permission* in order to do it. You can do it today.

Decision Analysis – Dr. Karl Misulis

We made our decisions, and we have our outcomes. Now it is time to analyze our choices. Why do we do this? We do it because we need to determine whether our decision-making is on-target, valid, or flawed and needs a redesign for future decisions. Perhaps we might be able to take a step back and fix the outcome of the decision under question.

To illustrate this process, we will analyze my own decision-making process as I applied it to my own life and career. I have come a long way and made many good decisions, and a few for which I would like a do-over. Young Karl was a bright, imperfect child who was not so different from most on our planet, with many possibilities for the future, some more realistic than others. I decided I wanted a career in medicine. There are different ways to do it in medicine, but a significant branching point is to be a scientist or practicing physician. These are related but very different in workflow and lifestyle, And there are a few people who do both, spend part of their effort doing clinical medicine and part doing research. That blend seemed exciting to me, so that was my decision. I got an undergraduate degree from Queen's University in Canada, a medical degree, MD, from Vanderbilt University in Tennessee, and a scientist degree, Ph.D., from the State University of New York. Armed with those credentials, I was ready to take on the world. Time to get a job. But which position do I want? Would I be the full-time scientist, the full-time physician, or the rare but exciting physician-scientist, doing both? At that time,

I chose the latter. I didn't think about it much, I was prepared for that job, so I was going to give it a go.

What if I had done a formal pre-decision analysis? Which would have been the logical choice? It depends on what parameters we want to use to measure success. So let's step back in time and do that.

All three of these possibilities are hard, and sustainability is very different. Getting enough patients to make a good living as a physician is very easy. Even the last person in the medical school class did well. However, science is complicated and depends on getting grants which are tricky. So here are the numbers.

A pure physician has a 95% chance of making a lucrative career. A small number, less than 5%, is not successful, either through personality quirks, being too picky about their situation, or just deciding to quit medicine. A pure medical scientist has a 34% chance of getting grant after grant and getting academic advancement to stay in the game. The rest leave to form or join a business or leave science altogether. That is not a happy statistic. The physician-scientist, blending clinical medicine and research into a long-term career, is even worse, 20%. The other 80% who try this path cannot do both well, so they flip to one or the other, science or medicine, and in that case, usually medicine.

I took that physician-scientist path, thinking I might be one of that 20%. I knew the odds were against me, but I wanted to take my shot. I missed. So, now I am a physician and not a research scientist. I do other things like teaching and writing, but being a physician pays the bills. Did I make the wrong decision? No. I know the odds were against me. But I wanted that physician-scientist role. I did my best, but my best was not good enough, at least my best without giving up on family and fun. It didn't work out, so I went to plan B and am happy. That was my decision-making and decision analysis.

Now, let us consider a person considering their first or subsequent job opportunity and making a decision with a simple branch point. One branch is starting a business. The other branch is becoming an employee of an existing company. Before making our decision, we must decide the measures of our success. There are two key performance indicators or KPIs for someone looking for or starting a job. One is monetary compensation, we need to be revenue positive at some point, and different positions offer different positivity; we cannot go our entire lives revenue negative. Another KPI is personal satisfaction. Are we happy and fulfilled with what we are doing? So, our personal KPIs are income and satisfaction, and we will make our choice depending on our estimate of what those KPI outcomes will be if we either start a business or become one employee. Can we predict how our KPIs will turn out? To a certain extent, we can have data for other people since millions have started businesses and billions have become employees.

As we look at data, let us first promise to minimize our biases. We are not necessarily smarter or harder working than many others, so while those attributes will affect our success, let us not assume we are gifted or entitled. Let us be objective.

What is the data? We have numbers on those exact KPIs. The numbers are a little dirty because the financial success data is from the US market and the personal satisfaction data is from Europe. However, that is still the best we have, and I have combined data from more than one study and rounded the numbers, but here we go.

First, for monetary compensation, if someone becomes an employee, they have a 90% chance of getting the expected income. About 10% did not, and we don't know whether that is because they dreamed they would get more, felt trapped in a low-paying job, or were being cheated. The data can't tell us that. For the business starter, the chance of the business being open after one year is 60%, the chance of being revenue positive is 30% in the first year, and 40% in the business's lifetime. Ouch! But before we all decide to be employees, let's look at the satisfaction data. Of the employee, about 50% have positive satisfaction, more satisfied than not. The other 50% are content with their job but not personally satisfied as they might have wished. For a startup business, the satisfaction is 80%. Why would that be? Because there are elements to satisfaction other than money, between the excitement of building and designing a business and taking their shot, the satisfaction far exceeds financial success. Of course, we cannot pay our electric bills with satisfaction, so either the business-starter is one of the 40% who becomes sustainable, or at some point, they step back and consider taking another shot at another business or decide to be an employee.

This is parallel to my career. I took my shot at a low-probability-of-success opportunity. I missed it, switched to Plan B, and I am happy. I do not (often) think of what might have been, and I have no regrets about the time and effort I put into taking that shot. The point here is that I am glad that I tried to shoot for the moon. It did not work out, but I took my fall-back plan and am satisfied.

Where does this take us on decision analysis? First, we do our homework. For our critical decisions, we make sure we know the possible outcomes. We place a value on each of those outcomes as possible. Determine what our KPIs are going to be. Make a decision and go with it. When we have interim or final results, see how they stack up on the KPIs. When these data are actionable, apply the same rigorous decision to whether we should take some new or alternative action. Perhaps we can change the outcome. Perhaps not.

Second, we see how we did about decision-making. We will make countless vital decisions in our lives, so ensure we make those decisions wisely. Were we objective and informed about making our KPIs? Did we make the best effort? A common failure method is getting off to a good start and then coasting to the finish line, a losing strategy. Third, apply what we learned through this experience to our next major decision.

SECTION 3: ONCE YOU GET THERE, HOW TO BE HAPPY

Cognitive Limits – Dr. Karl Misulis

We hate to think about the possibility of cognitive limits. We assume that we have magnificent infinite intellectual powers; but unfortunately, that assumption is often proven wrong. It might seem depressing to consider that we have limits, but we must deal with them, and this is just part of our personal self-delusion that we have infinite powers.

Most of us believe we have above-average intelligence; 94% of us, in fact. In another study, 80% of us believe we have above-average romantic performance. Our consumption of fiction makes our self-delusion even worse with depictions of unlimited mental power and success with sheer will, which of course, is sheer fantasy. There are case reports, of sometimes superhuman performance. Some are true, but others are exaggerated. Some are hyperbole, and often incorrect, either through analysis or falsification. My point is that I don't want anyone to be depressed by highlighting our limitations. I do want us to be aware of our limitations so we can realistically deal with them.

The Number Of Variables That We Can Consider

A famous scientist studied the number of simultaneous variables that a person could comprehend, and that number is about seven. Even then, if there are different weights to some of the variables, each one of those weights is a variable itself. So, the number of independent variables people can handle is usually far less than seven. The trouble is that most complex systems have far more than seven variables. In fact, almost all of them do. So, how do we deal with that limitation?

There's only one choice: to *reduce the set of variables* down to a number and a type that we can consider. How do we do that? One of the ways that we often use is to pick a few variables that we can measure and understand. You might pick the wrong ones, though, so we need to make sure we pick the right ones that are important. Alternatively, sometimes we can cascade variables. For example, suppose we have a project, and there are multiple different parts of that project. In that case, we could not understand all of the variables of all of the systems, but we might be able to understand it better if each component had one super-important variable. For example, say we are building an engine prototype, and there is someone in charge of the fuel system, someone in charge of temperature control, etc. We would get the fuel person to give us all their variables distilled down into one or two small variables that we can understand, and we do the same thing for the temperature control system and for the torque output system. There are so many of these that we can only consider just the very few that we have selected. So that's one way of dealing with it

Revisionist Memory

This is another one of our problems. Remember Ronald Reagan? As a campaigning politician, he would tell an anecdote about an event he had heard that occurred during World War II. Early on, he told the story as it had been told to him, and then over time, he told the story as if he had been a direct observer, and then over more time, he told the same story as if he had been one of the key characters in the story. He was not lying. his mind gradually rearranged the story to his personal advantage.

How do we avoid this? We can't, totally. We could keep a diary of important events. I do that, but a chief way is to admit the fuzziness of memory. I might say, "I believe I saw __" to make our point unless I am absolutely certain of the facts.

Tendency To Believe That We Are Unbreakable

"Unbreakable" was a movie starring Bruce Willis. He could not get hurt. He'd be in a train wreck, and everybody else would get killed except for him. We see video clips, real or fake, of death-defying stunts and events, so we assume that we will survive similar actions. Until it is proved otherwise, we feel ourselves to be immortal.

So how do we fight this? We remember our injuries and those of loved ones. Serious injury or death of a close friend really should remind us that we are vulnerable. And remember, many death-defying videos and all action adventure movies are not true.

Deflecting Responsibility

It is human nature not to take direct responsibility for something bad that happens to ourselves or to others secondary to our actions or inactions. It is a psychological defense mechanism. Otherwise, we would be forever paralyzed by guilt for our actions. So how do we protect against deflection yet avoid guilt paralysis? The best way is to accept responsibility and then try to make it better in some way. We often cannot totally make up for the fallout, but we should try, and often just the admission of responsibility gives relief to ourselves and someone we might have hurt by our actions.

Well, these are just some of the ways that we live with our cognitive limits. The most important part of this talk is that we learn to heighten our awareness of them. We must be aware of our biases, our faults, our self-serving actions, and our self-serving memories. We rely on our introspective minds and those of our friends to help get us through life.

Dealing With Crazies - Dr. Karl Misulis

Let's discuss how to deal with crazies. Of course, this is a provocative title. What we really mean is how do we deal with those who make irrational decisions? The Merriam-Webster definition of "crazy" is "marked by thought or action that lacks reason." And that is the definition we are referring to.

Some of our other writings deal with how other people and we make irrational decisions due to cognitive biases or logical flaws. Their nonscientific approach might not be evident until they have communicated quite a bit. Even some irrational thoughts can have some plausible foundations. But there are some simple observations that give us a clue to the lack of a scientific approach.

People Who Decide To Prove A Specific Finding Are Irrational

This is where they announce that they are attempting to prove their belief. I recall a documentary where a couple of amateur scientists reported that they knew that the Bimini Road, a geologic formation in the Bahamas, was man-made and was Atlantis, and they were going to prove it! No, no. That is not how science works. We make observations and do experiments, and based on those results, we develop our beliefs, which we test further. Either it is man-made or not. Either it is Atlantis or not. By the way, for reference, the Bimini road is a natural formation and is not the site of Atlantis. Plato did not get to the western hemisphere.

People Who Spend More Time Talking Than Listening Are Often Passing On Information Of Dubious Value.

Few of us can talk continuously without being repetitive or inventive.

People admired, wealthy, or otherwise well respected are not correct by definition. In fact, with people hanging on their every word, they often tend to join their followers in believing everything they say.

More subtly, we tend to believe a plausible explanation. I know what you are thinking, "If it is plausible, it is most likely true." This is an understandable point of view but flawed. Science experiments test whether one or another potentially plausible explanation for a phenomenon is correct. An example is the disappearance of a puddle of water in a depression on solid rock. The puddle could evaporate, or it could soak into the porous surface of the rock, or someone could have dried the surface. All of these are plausible, and more than one might be correct, but not necessarily so, and probably not all are correct.

How Do We Deal With Irrational Thoughts?

An example might be someone who believes that the Earth is flat, a flat-earther. Separately from the spoilsports who say that the Earth being flat fills one definition where the layers are parallel, and indeed they are, in the absence of bumps and dips, since all layers of the Earth are affected by the curvature of the Earth. Over contiguous atoms, a vector between two adjacent atoms is parallel to a vector between two atoms a layer down. No, we mean that the Earth is flat like ancient representations, like a cheap pizza.

So, Bubba says, "The earth is flat." A response such as "Moron, your brain is flat" will not convince Bubba.

Rather, first, identify with Bubba and his thought process. "Yes, I've heard that. Tell me the logic behind that." Listen to the arguments, offer alternative explanations, and then explore together satellite images, flight plans, and horizon effects and come to a different conclusion. You both together refute the theory.

So you have taught Bubba that the Earth is not flat, in the classical sense, and have taught Bubba a skill on how to investigate statements.

Before we close, we need to be a scientist and consider the possibility of being the crazy ones. We might, at times, make irrational decisions. So, remember that we are not the smartest person on the planet. And even the smartest person makes mistakes. We should examine our thought processes. Do we hold irrational views? Do we make irrational decisions?

We are wrong if we conclude that every idea coming from a particular person or group is correct or incorrect. We are being irrational. No person or group is completely right or wrong. We cannot abrogate our truth meters based on our emotions.

So, the moral of the story is to *be rational, use reason, and think analytically*. In short, be the scientist.

Why The Corporate Landscape Is Full Of Bad Bosses – Eliana Silbermann

Nowadays, managers who are "bad" in the sense of being outright tyrants, dictators, or monsters don't usually last long. But the other kind of bad—managers who are incompetent, weak, overstretched, and miserable? It seems we've all worked for one. They're an endless trope in movies, TV, and books.

Why is it so easy to find terrible managers?

The Peter Principle

In 1969, Dr. Laurence Johnston Peter published a book with an explanation. He stated that "in a hierarchy, every employee tends to rise to his level of incompetence." Many companies promote employees who are good at their jobs and have been there the longest. These employees continue to be promoted until they get stuck in a job they're not good at.

Most people find jobs based on technical or specialized skills. For example, computer programmers, accountants, or salespeople. But management requires a completely separate skillset. It's a different career.

There's another layer to the Peter Principle. Being incompetent in a job makes most people miserable. As the cliché goes, misery loves company. Unhappy people tend to make the people around them unhappier (sometimes, but not always, deliberately).

Becoming A Manager For The Wrong Reasons

In many companies, employees don't have alternative paths to getting pay raises or advancing their careers. Some people want the power of being the boss solely to fulfill their own needs. Or their new title represents status and prestige. These new managers don't enjoy the role and aren't equipped to lead their teams. Some companies fall victim to the Peter Principle. Other companies promote or hire managers based entirely on nepotism—favoring family members or friends—or workplace politics. Nepotism isn't automatically bad, but it should never be the only criterion.

Not Enough Support For New Managers

Most managers get between zero and two days of training for their new role. The trouble is that management is its career. Some people will already have the required abilities and skills. Even so, they need guidance and support. They're thrown into the deep end to figure out their new leadership responsibilities. No one shows them how to set expectations, the right way to give feedback (whether positive or negative), and how to address poor performance or delegate tasks. They lack confidence in navigating difficult situations that require advanced interpersonal skills, problem-solving, or expert planning.

Signs Of A Bad Manager

Here are a few characteristics and behaviors to watch out for:

- Lack of compassion or empathy
- Micromanaging
- Inflexible
- Unwilling to compromise
- Yelling at employees
- Knee jerk reactions
- Flip-flopping on decisions or not making decisions
- Playing favorites
- Workaholic

What Can You Do?

While good effective managers are similar, bad manager tends to do their job poorly in their unique way. Still, there are ways to deal with ineffective or counterproductive bosses. If your boss is disorganized, forgetful, or doesn't care much

Create a team calendar for meetings, deadlines, and separate concurrent projects. Make your reports as simple as possible. Keep room in your schedule for emergencies. If your boss is controlling, doesn't trust their team, or is overcritical

Update your manager about your project before they ask. Lay out each team member's responsibilities. Achieve product goals to win their trust.

If your boss fosters a competitive work environment and measures individual performance instead of seeing projects as a team effort

Encourage your colleagues to collaborate instead of compete. Start group conversations face to face, via email, or by video. Discuss team goals. Receive written approval and directions in writing for project expectations and plans. If your boss comes up with lots of ideas but never follows through, distracts not only themself but everyone else, and makes spur-of-the-moment decisions

Suggest realistic deadlines. Ask them to prioritize each idea, and have honest discussions about whether there's enough time or energy for quality work. Suggest ways to increase productivity and improve efficiency. Ask whether their new ideas will help or hurt team goals and the bottom line.

Yes, you might be taking over some of your boss's responsibilities. Sometimes there's not much else you can do—if you can't or don't want to look for a new job. There's some good news. If and when you decide to move on, your CV and LinkedIn page will be packed with juicy impressive bullet points. You'll have plenty of eargrabbing stories for interviewers.

Never complain about, criticize, or insult your boss to potential new employers. Focus on your accomplishments and describe the context of the situation tactfully.

Bullshit, Lies, And Other Nonsense - Dr. Karl Misulis

Perhaps the term bullshit is not politically correct for professional writing, but the term captures this topic perfectly. Bullshit, otherwise known as BS, is information someone conveys that is judged untrue from the recipient's point of view. It does not say anything about what the speaker thinks; they might know it's false or not. On the other hand, a lie is a deliberate misinformation that the speaker knows to be incorrect. So, a lie is where the speaker believes the information to be wrong. BS is where the listener believes the information to be inaccurate. More than a subtle difference.

Before we get into the motivations and mechanisms, let's consider why we would encounter these entities in our modern business and personal discourse. We can all imagine or recall an instance, but let's look at a few examples. Manager: "Hey [insert slimy name here], Did you finish that report on Bullshit for Misulis Group?" Slimy: "Yes, I did a great job, but then my dog ate my report." Manager: "So your dog ate your laptop?" Slimy: "I wrote it on my phone, and the dog ate my phone." Manager: "So bring the dog here, and when it defecates your phone, we will see which is crappier, the dog or the writing." Misulis Group managers can be tough.

Slimy told a lie, a statement he knew to be untrue. The manager identified Slimy's statement as bullshit, presuming it was a lie. There is a minimal chance that the dog could have eaten the phone, and an even smaller chance that the report could be on the phone, so we do not need to be 100% sure to judge something as BS. We can speak from likelihood.

Here is one more example with a twist. Manager: "Can you finish that report up tonight? Slimy: "Sure thing. I'll have it in your inbox by 8:00 am." Manager: "Great, we have to have it uploaded by 9:00 am." Slimy promised he would have it done, but he thought it would be early enough to finish by 10:00 am. He lied to get some more time, telling the manager what he wanted to hear, yet had no intention of completing the project. The manager told Slimy that it had to be uploaded by 9:00 am when it did not need to be uploaded until 5:00 pm. So a series of needless lies occurred. What happened here? Slimy had a history of being late with work, so the manager had developed the habit of giving early deadlines. Slimy had learned this, so he had developed the habit of turning in his work even later. It would usually be completed barely in time. This workflow was acceptable for this brief example but should not have occurred. Some managers and businesses would not tolerate this, and Slimy would be looking for a new job. Most businesses and organizations do not have the time and patience for this kind of scenario. Most personal relationships should not have to suffer from this type of interaction.

Why Don't We Have Total Honesty In Our Work And Personal Lives?

Part of the answer is the difference between present and future value. In this context, we are not talking about money. We are talking about the emotional currency of the individuals we are dealing with. Present value is our intended impact on the person we are talking to. Future value is the future impact on the person and their relationship with us. For the first example, Slimy does not want the manager to get mad at him, so he lies. He is less likely to get fired with this lie than if he told the truth that he was too lazy to finish it on time. He discounts the future value of the manager's opinion of him. He assumes the most significant threat is the discourse during the immediate interaction, and he needs to save face if possible.

For the second example, the manager has learned that Slimy will be late, so he gives him a deadline earlier than the real one. Slimy makes promises to the manager that he does not intend to keep. He knows from experience that the deadline is artificially early and that being a little late will be okay. This dance works for this duo, but badly. Neither has the trust of the other.

Why do people lie? We may be induced to tell lies because we want an immediate favorable reaction. We might also tell lies to produce an emotional response from our colleagues. Almost always, it is an attempt to raise their opinion of us. We might want to convey a message that makes us look bold, strong, or knowledgeable. Whether we carry good or bad news, there is respect for someone who gives information our brain considers essential. In our quest to share interesting information with others, we might listen to someone's lie, believe it, and then tell it to another. At that point, we are not lying since we are not intentionally giving misinformation. Our listener may correctly judge our statement as false, in which case it is BS, though not a lie. How do we detect BS?

When told something unbelievable, I sometimes say, "My BS detector just sounded." While that is a joke, it is an announcement of disbelief. It's a version of someone saying, "Really? That is hard to believe." Or a softer version might be, "Are you sure that is true?"

Our minds do have a BS detector of sorts. Our mind assesses incoming information and determines how that information syncs with what we already know or believe. Our memory is relational, meaning we do not remember everything like a computer. We create and modify memories that are topically related to each other. So our new memories have to be reconciled with our stored memories and opinions. That little voice in the back of our mind, which tells us that a statement is untrue, is not always, but often correct. The information is a lie, BS, or a new authentic item that deserves to be remembered and influences our future judgments.

We can be a bit more scientific about BS detection. One clue is the volume of the surprising statements. If an individual is renowned for coming up with one unbelievable thing after another, and the spheres of each are far different, such as medicine to geology, then it's usually BS. When do we challenge?

If we know the statement is BS, we could call them out on it, but that often sours the relationship between the parties. It can sometimes develop into an argument over the facts, which may not get resolved in the absence of a definitive source. This serves to produce bad feelings on both sides. An alternative approach depends on how important the statement is. If we are pretty sure it is untrue, options include: Nothing — giving little or no response will tell the speaker that the information is in an area of disinterest or unbelievable but does not specify which. Also, the reinforcement to the speaker of an emotional response from the listener is absent.

Mild Challenge — Perhaps something friendlier such as, "That is so surprising, let's look that up to see if it's true."

Moderate Challenge — If we are more confident that the statement is not true, we might say something like, "That sounds like nonsense. Who told you that? They'd have to convince me." The attack is on a mythical person as a source.

Severe Challenge — If we are pretty confident that the statement is untrue, we might make an in-their-face challenge; "That is total bullshit." However, we do not recommend using that approach. Both sides are angry, and the speaker usually does not change their behavior from this. They get defensive, often alienating us from them, and do not check their facts. We might think this approach will induce them to check their sources, but this rarely occurs.

How do we make mistakes in our truth analytics? In this discussion, we have assumed that we are the single source of truth, which is inaccurate. We often make mistakes in our judgments or statements, and we sometimes hold information to be factual when it is not. This is because of a host of cognitive biases discussed in another part of this book. One of these pertinent to this discussion is a form of Implicit Bias called InGroup Bias. We believe what people in a group we identify with say with little or no questioning. It tends to make us believe what we want and disbelieve uncomfortable or dissonant statements. Don't do that. I know what you are thinking, "I'm not like that. I am a perfectly rational analytic person and assess every statement on its merits." No, you're not, and no, you don't. None of us are.

But we should aspire to be that individual and do our best to be objective.

What Is The Approach To Handling Potential BS?

The approaches to handling lies and BS are critical since many beliefs are closely held and have no factual foundation. Whether it be related to election outcomes or vaccine effects, we have good data, yet those data are called BS, and the callers are actually the ones producing the BS and often lie. How do we handle potential BS?

First, determine whether it is a statement that needs to be checked and if it is relatively harmless and inconsequential, let it go, and ignore it. Second, if it needs to be checked, do our research. This might be asking knowledgeable individuals, consulting reference material, or simply web-searching the topic. But be careful, don't let the bias of even published material mislead you. Third, if important enough to confront the misinformation, challenge the deliverer.

Many topics are so inconsequential that we can just smile and say, "That's surprising," and then move on in the conversation. Again, don't give the emotional response or attention the speaker wants. Not every fact needs to be challenged. If we do, we will have no friends. We challenge when it is mission-critical, either by the material's importance or the speaker's veracity in future encounters.

How Do We Keep From Promulgating Lies?

How do we not tell lies? Don't do it. We are most likely to tell lies when we want to impress or deceive. There are better ways to impress, and there is seldom a need to deceive. Lying and deceiving might produce favorable short-term results but have real and almost certain long-term negative consequences for us.

We are most likely to re-send lies when we do not do our homework. If data is important enough to re-transmit, make sure it is accurate.

When exaggerating, we are sometimes on the border zone between true and false. Some of us are prone to hyperbole, as I am. In speaking and writing, I sometimes use hyperbole where the intent is to exaggerate to the extent that it is not believable yet makes a point. I might say something like, "Edison had more than a million inventions." Actually, the number was a bit less. Both those statements are hyperbole. You know that he did not have a million inventions and also know that the number was not a bit less but a lot less. But I made the point that he invented a lot of stuff. If I instead make the statement "Edison had more than a thousand patents," that is probably hyperbole also, but it is almost believable. Hyperbole needs to be obvious and not to be judged as a lie. By the way, the answer was 1,093 US patents, so 1000 was about right. Isn't that unbelievable?

How Do We Avoid Promulgating BS?

In this context, how do we not relay suspect information? First, we use our BS detector, as already discussed. We should check surprising statements for accuracy before acting on or telling them to others. How much checking is needed? If a person or a publication is generally reliable, such as NPR, then say, "I heard on NPR that...".

If there is some doubt about the information, another method is to introduce the doubt in our statement, such as by saying, "I saw this on NPR...". That way, if the information is ultimately found to be untrue, you are not judged to be the source of untruth. We all have tremendous assets and some liabilities. None of us is perfect. But we should strive to be factual as much as possible.

We must avoid being anchored into believing information just because we like the individual or entity projecting the info.

We should be the reliable source, the one who checks important data or gives disclaimers if we are unsure. We never grant complete veracity to any friend, relative, group, political party, or other individual or body of individuals. We need to be free-thinkers, not puppets of groups, media, or other individuals.

ABOUT THE AUTHORS

Christie Hawking is an all-rounder content writer. No topic is off the table, and a challenge is always welcomed. Taking life as it comes, change is something she takes head-on. Her life is far from monotonous, frolicking around the world while she attained four degrees. She holds an International master's in security, Intelligence, and Strategic Studies. She also has degrees in psychology, criminology, and public policy. Following a single path or learning one topic is never enough. Always looking on the bright side of life, she has no time for negativity.

Sophiko Lagvilava has more than 8 years' experience with both national and international organisations. She's always looking for new ways to solve problems, and specialises in business communication, relationship management, and team/professional development. She completed her Bachelor of Journalism and Master of Journalism degrees at Ivane Javakhishvili State University of Tbilisi. Sophiko lives in Tbilisi, Georgia where she spends her free time following sumo wrestling matches.

Rachel Langston is an artist, educator, and woman on a quest to find the best job. She writes about everything wrong with the corporate world and why it's terrible. She holds two bachelor's degrees from the University of North Texas and served in the Peace Corps in Georgia. Rachel lives in Tbilisi, Georgia, with her husband, son, and two Siamese cats.

Karl Edward Misulis is a physician, scientist, educator, and university professor. He has a BSc From Queen's University Canada, MD from Vanderbilt University, and Ph.D. from SUNY Syracuse. He has authored over 20 books, some in multiple languages, and lectured worldwide to the public and fellow academics.

KC Misulis, Founder and CEO of Misulis Group OÜ, has over a decade of management consulting experience. He has worked on projects on four continents, focusing on SME development. He is committed to empowering workers and creating strong work-life balance within organizations.

Eliana Silbermann writes about work to help you create a career that's the garlic to your bread. She believes that work should fit into your life instead of your life squeezing around your job. When she's not clickety clacking on her keyboard, she plays snooker and bakes eggy bread.

If you liked the articles in here and want to read articles just like these, check us out at MisulisGroup.com

www.ingramcontent.com/pod-product-compliance
Lightning Source LLC
LaVergne TN
LVHW010356160826
845677LV00005BA/1298

* 9 7 9 8 3 6 6 6 4 8 9 9 8 *